Overland Park

poetry and flash fiction

by Michael Malan

BLUE LIGHT PRESS ◆ 1ST WORLD PUBLISHING

1st WORLD
PUBLISHING

SAN FRANCISCO ◆ FAIRFIELD ◆ DELHI

1ST WORLD LIBRARY
PO Box 2211
Fairfield, IA 52556
www.1stworldpublishing.com

BLUE LIGHT PRESS
www.bluelightpress.com
Email: bluelightpress@aol.com

BOOK & COVER DESIGN
Melanie Gendron
www.melaniegendron.com

COVER ART
Making the Run to Gladewater by Jeanne Williams

AUTHOR PHOTOGRAPH
Roberta Sperling

FIRST EDITION

Library of Congress Control Number: 2017932139

ISBN 9781421837734

Poems in this book have previously appeared in the following publications:

Poetry East: "Alms for the Poor," "How to Amuse a Tree"
Rosebud: "Moses—The Early Years," "Just Like Paul Bunyan"
Oregon Literary Review: "The Moving House"
Rhino: "A Grim Appearance," "Lemon Twist"
Heliotrope: "Once I Was a Spider-Man," "Handrail of the Stars,"
    "What Large Eyes"
Hawaii Review: "Titan's Blue Aura"
Epoch: "The Advance Gardening Memoranda"
Coe Review: "Close the Door"
Portland Review: "Restless Spirit," "The End of Time,"
    "Between the Body and the Window is Another Revelation,"
    "A New Language"
The South Carolina Review: "Wrong Number," "Why I Like War"
Blue Earth Review: "New Friends"
North Chicago Review: "Strange Artifacts"
Kestrel: "Only in Dreams"
Wisconsin Review: "A Really Good Smoke," "Turnpike"
Solo Novo: "The Glass Tulip," "Reflections on the Revolution
    in California"
Hayden's Ferry Review: "Mutant High School,"
    "Falling Birds," "Having a Good Time"
CutBank: "Overland Park"
Bayou: "Agents of the Prince"
Denver Quarterly: "I Don't Know If It's Cloudy or Bright"
The Potomac Review: "American Spirit"
Miramar: "Broken-Hearted Melodies"
Cutthroat: "War of Independence"
Borderlands: Texas Poetry Review: "The Man Who Fell in the River"

for my parents

CONTENTS

I. Are All Parties Like This?

II. A Question Mark in a Forest of Snowflakes

III. Red Poppies on the Moon

I. Are All Parties Like This?

Mi Amiga Favorita

I tried almost everything: climbing the Taj
Mahal, thinking like a friendly dog,
falling asleep in the Tunnel of Love.
Then I realized that what
you wear doesn't matter so much as what you
say: most red roosters are on fire.
In a nearby town they are painting angels on the
police station. Look, there's a dog with a transmitting
device. Officer Pup.
In India they have an unusual viewpoint.
How different our lives are now that we are free.

Two things that happened: the Super Moon got so
heavy it fell from the sky
like a pancake. Nothing is too dangerous
for the laundry boys. In another age
they will discover how flight really works.
Two men who know each
other very well will disappear in broad daylight.
When I whistle, ships haul anchor. We were not
required to read Byron in school. In Spanish class,
mi amiga favorita was Gertrude Stein. I am
desperate for a new world order.

A Grim Appearance

You give a glass of whiskey to your enemies
to disarm them, whether they are naked or
dressed in snow and flowers like Himalayan
ogres. All this stuff about things as they are is
good, but what are they? What animates them?
On the way home I imagined
a doughnut stopping for coffee, getting his head
stuck in the cup. "Hey, amigo," he said to the waiter,
"help me out." Night fell with latté swiftness.
A grim appearance, muchacho, lit the highway.

Restless Spirit

His Mustang is parked alongside Highway 89 outside
Great Falls, Montana. The sky, like the car, is metallic
blue. He is wearing a white shirt and smiling like he just
thought of something funny. He reminds you of someone
you knew before, a man with a large penis. In a photograph
he is nude, obviously proud of his penis, lying on the roof
of a low, wooden building. Two people, sitting nearby,
wear Santa Claus masks. You place your jewelry in a glass
dish beside your bed. You look out the window. Snow
is falling, huge flakes like saucers of milk. We are no longer
mistress and slave, you think, as he steps back from the bed
and snaps your picture. Tonight the moon is drifting in a lake
of passion. Next to beauty what is truth? Ice melts, a small
bruise appears on your thigh. You sit on the floor, light
a candle. Beads of light trail in the dust.

I Don't Know If It's Cloudy or Bright

Before I fall asleep,
Adele comes to tuck me in.
Talk and tuck. She is on the wagon,
she tells me, then off again.
He hit me, no he didn't.
Our neighbors are shape-shifting reptiles.
Kennedy killed Oswald, not the other way around.
Father: What are you up to? Adele: Page 77.
Only the broom is the true idea.
God is something else. Love maybe.
Confetti. The world as fact and the world
as fiction—how else can we explain
all these miraculous transformations?
Before Wittgenstein and Kierkegaard
there were radical shadows on nearly every
building. Robots slogging through a mist.
The machine in the gray flannel suit.
Try to remember. You were walking away,
into another life—the dog bit the car.
I only had eyes for someone else.

A Really Good Smoke

Smokey Robinson on the radio, singing
a sweet, lowdown tune. Governors
massing at the statehouse,
our own governor fishing for steelheads
at Lake Okabogee. I used to wear jeans
and boots like he does, back in the days
when I had a lot to prove. I was a solitary man,
a swineherd on the hogback.

Yesterday, I wrote a couple of bad poems,
then went to the poetry store to sell them.
No takers, so I went to a pawn shop
and traded the poems for a magical cigar box
with a picture of Don Juan Ortega y Gasset
on the cover. Don Juan was a minor poet
in seventeenth-century Peru,
a strong man for the junta that was

eventually snuffed out by descendants
of Chief Mazatlán, a cigar smoker
of the first magnitude. Tonight,
I am lying in a hammock looking at a bizarre
constellation in the northern sky, near
where Orion normally stands, holding his club
like a Neanderthal. A shooting star
rips through the treetops.

Broken-Hearted Melodies

1. And There I Was, Walking Down the Street

I was listening to a song by Pat Boone, a tune from a long time ago. It wasn't "April Love," but something else, a river with an attitude, or a beach where dreams are washed away. That's how it was then. The muse came and went. She hid in a crowd on a busy street or in a small house on the banks of a moody river. And when she left, I cried for a long time. A few years later, at the hop, I was starting to feel better. Leaping and dancing, I felt like Nureyev—or the fiddler on the roof.

2. Oh, Baby

She gave me her ring, but it wasn't enough. I had an appointment, something I dread. It wasn't the witch doctor so much as his sidekick, Igor, and those baying hounds. Should I pawn the ring? It didn't seem right to keep it. Maybe I would leave it outside in the rain. Or maybe I would just watch TV. *I Love Lucy* or *The Addams Family*—it was all the same to me. Just last week, we were playing Kiss & Tell. One of the girls had the best lips, mysterious. There was a hint of a promise, a seduction later, as we stood outside the ancient temple and rolled cigarettes. Karnak, 1963, and I held the mummy's breath in my hand.

3. Like Life

We were traveling the highways and byways, so happy together. Then she left me standing by the road—and I was hitchhiking through the mountains and across the plains, listening to Johnny Mathis sing one of my favorite songs. I cried all the way home. My dog was glad to see me, but most of my friends had left town. And now, as I write this, blue shadows seem to follow one another across the plains. And the mountains are so full of themselves. Like life, the great sad time is upon me.

4. Face to Face

Tonight, I am listening to *Abbey Road*, which, oddly enough, passes in front of my house. Yesterday, I was playing darts with Jumpin' Jack Flash. Tomorrow, I'll take a ferry across the Mersy, drink tea with Mrs. Brown's lovely daughter, or just feel glad all over. The lights on the Christmas tree have come undone. I am flashing on and off, like a Roman candle. At night, when the stars are dim, I come face to face with who I really am.

5. Tomorrow

Was I blue. Nothing seemed to work out. Every way I turned, some obstacle appeared. An ode I didn't understand, a souvenir of the last glad time. I was off to join the circus, the world seemed cruel. I played the Up & Down Club with the Big Show Band, changed my name to Del. I got my break in 1962 with Lawrence Welk in Calcutta, midnight on the Ganges. Then Cairo, Illinois, for a stint in the magic carpet business. When I was 34, I sold the family farm and worked for a pioneer radio station in the Midwest. A DJ for the drifters, I was twisting my life away. Tomorrow came suddenly.

Mutant High School

Eating lunch in the high school cafeteria, I noticed that all my classmates were weird. Some had overly large heads and arms that hung nearly to the ground. Others had long necks like giraffes. A few were obese and walked about on all fours, snorting like rhinoceroses.

When I got home that night I asked my dad about the school. "All the kids are mutants," I complained. "They don't seem human. I don't know how to explain it."

My dad was sitting on the couch watching TV. "Have a seat," he said, one eye on *Famous Home Videos*. I sat down and looked at the TV. Deeply tanned nude people were splashing in an enormous kidney-shaped pool.

"So you think the kids are mutants," Dad said, watching a beautiful blonde climb up on a diving board.

"Yeah," I said. "They're all really weird. They're like part human, part animal."

"Inbreeding," Dad said, still looking at the tube. "Do you know what that is?

"Yeah, it's like having sex with your brother or sister."

"Not exactly," he said. "Why don't you look it up."

Inbreeding.com was a trip. There were pictures of people like the kids at school, except they were middle-aged and had won prestigious awards. A few had been beauty queens on distant planets. Others belonged to a secret society called the X-Persons, who were, according to the website, "engaged in a war against the forces of evil."

The next day at school I saw things differently. I was more tolerant of the other kids. I started dating a girl who had silver-white hair and dark, stormy eyes. But eventually she dropped me for someone who looked just like her.

Falling Birds

It was so cold birds were freezing and falling from the sky. "Be careful of those falling birds," my mother said.

I peeked out the door, the sky was clear, so I ran down the street to the bus shelter. Once I was inside, frozen birds fell mercilessly on the roof. *Thump! Thump!*

Some of the younger kids were scared. One little boy started crying. "I want my mommy," he said.

"Shut up!" one of the other kids said, but I could tell he was scared, too. His teeth were chattering and he had that haunted, frozen-bird look in his eye.

One of the girls spoke to the boys tenderly: "Don't be afraid," she said. "The birds are not heavy enough to smash the shelter." Just as she said that, a frozen eagle hit the roof and we heard an ominous, splintering sound.

The youngest boy was sobbing, and I figured I better do something quick, so I prayed. "Dear Mother Nature," I said, "please save us from the falling birds." There was a long silence and the school bus pulled up to the shelter. We jumped on the bus and rode to school without incident.

That afternoon, the temperature rose and we all returned home safely.

"Was it a miracle?" I asked my mother.

"I don't know," she said. "I'm just glad you're home safe." She wrapped her arms around me like wings. And my dad sat on the couch like a hawk.

Having a Good Time

Janeen didn't get out much—going to a party was a big deal. She spent hours putting on makeup, combing her hair, selecting the right dress. Finally, she was ready. She felt like Cinderella in her special dress. This will be a wonderful party, she thought.

But when she got there she was disappointed. The party was dull. Men stood on one side of the room, women on the other. "Are all parties like this?" she asked one of the other women.

"Yes, isn't it great?" the woman said, her eyes shining.

Janeen looked at her carefully. She seemed different somehow, like she was high on drugs—or spirituality.

"Are you all right?" she asked the other woman.

"Oh, yes. I sure am," she said. "Why don't you try one of those brownies on the buffet table? Or read that little book on the bookshelf."

Janeen went to the bookshelf and picked up the book. It was entitled *Having a Good Time.* She opened the book and read the first few sentences. "There is no time, good or bad. Everything is happening in the Eternal Now. Eat the brownies."

She went to the buffet table, ate a brownie. The wall in front of her dissolved. She was standing at the edge of the solar system. Mars and Venus flashed past. She turned, stepped forward, everyone was her partner. The room moved through space like a waltz.

New Friends

It was like a trial balloon, so-and-so getting together. The notes
of violins drifted on the heavy air. Back from the north, she took
company seriously. The greenhouse moved closer. Something
about precious metals, hardy plants, sunshine in Spain or Amalfi.
In the distance a white beach dotted with red umbrellas. She
ordered a Perrier at the chromium bar. Large, trumpet-shaped
flowers nudged the bartender. Oldies. This was Florida. Time
had stopped. She was a different person now. You've outgrown
them, her father said. Find new friends.

Close the Door

Running or thinking. Another phone booth disappears.
A bridge between two ideas, an empty room, the bed
unmade. The room smaller than he remembered, half pink,
stationary, the word bark on the dog's mouth. Headlights
circling in the sky. They woke him up. Time to go. Down
to the station. The hospital. Bail him out. Run around town.
Language is another expression. Light snow falling. Heavy
wet snow in the nature of voice. Healing normal and natural.
Get the fear out of the way. Close the door, iron your pants.
The earth is humming. Breathing in, breathing out.

Overland Park

I decided to stop talking about it, a hand on the shoulder,
stack of green lawn chairs, a boy wearing a Halloween
mask or falling on his face laughing—the fence ran away
behind a row of houses—and now I know that something
else was on tap, amazing sleep and motion, not panic
or collateral damage, but the kind of sorrow that haunts
you when you find something priceless and it's taken
away, and your teacher tells you the cafeteria is off-limits,
and you want to say something, but it doesn't make sense,
it's not what you really feel—and learning how to express
those feelings is difficult, so you write letters to the editor,
and every page is like two ribbons of ink and every new
something is taken from the air like a diamond.

Only in Dreams

I.

I am dreaming about being a famous movie star,
falling in love with a tennis pro from Sweden
or Germany. Mother is not quite dead. Relatives
visit, tell me how I should live. Summer fades
in a smoky haze. I am holding each scene steady,
on my lap, on my laptop. My brother gestures
emphatically. "To the manor born," Grandpa
says, filling his pipe with tobacco. Someone's
shadow slips past the living room window.
I am driving home to get my things. Tomorrow
I will catch a plane for some place far away.
Change will come slowly, maybe take years.

II.

Everything is something else, not quite what
I thought it would be. I was dancing with
a young Lakota woman, then I was drunk,
hiding under my bed. Cars drifted like rivers
through smoke-lit streets. Mother and Father
fighting, then making up. Oncoming headlights
twisting the shadows of their heads on the roof
of the car. The last thing I remember: giant
faces on the movie screen blurred by rain.
We are going our separate ways. I am a wheel,
a truck, a fast car with eight cylinders. I am
sorry it is winter. I am a branch. I am a door.

III.

Third-world country. We are feeling the pinch.
No grape jelly, peanut butter, corn flakes,
cow's milk, or granulated sugar. I want to run
away from home, join the Brave Free Men.
Father is sipping bourbon and eating ice cream.
"A bourbon float," he jokes. A dark cloud passes
overhead, like in a Fifties science-fiction movie.
"There are many fish in the sea," he says to my
mother. But she loves only one. The man with
bushy black hair, the man from North Africa.
One day they will meet again, but not here; in
another world, she tells me, a place called Heaven.

IV.

I was restless, drinking whiskey, or riding a pony
on the reservation. My mother called me a liar.
I was listening to "Goodbye, Cruel World,"
a record I had stolen from a rich friend. "I will
not stay here another moment," Mother says.
Her cigarette bursts into flames. "Nat King Cole
died today," she says. Smoke unravels your spirit,
but it cannot unravel itself. We are driving home
between dog and wolf, the late hour, the latest
hour. We are considering a part-time job, a move
to a bigger city. Conversation lags. Only in dreams
do my hands open and close like dark lakes.

The Man Who Fell in the River

1

José fell into the Cheyenne River near Cherry Creek and drifted downstream for nearly ten miles. After he climbed from the river, he tried to signal for help with a chunk of mica he had found in a quarry not far from Thunder Butte and carried with him under his shirt, along with a photo of his dead wife, a woman who had treated him badly and acted as though their unhappy relationship was entirely his fault. He knew better. Their life together had been like a storm in a bottle, a shadow on their bedspread, an unfriendly relative from Guadalajara.

2

The night before he fell in the river, José was sitting in a bar in Juarez talking with a young anarchist who believed that Mexico was not a nation with sovereign borders and indigenous people. Mangy dogs crouched in the corners of the cantina. Strangers stood in rows at the bar demanding equal time with the Pope. "I have crossed the line into Texas only once," the young anarchist said, "and I found four vortexes: The Canyon of Twisted Rocks, The River of Mysterious Stars, The Isle of Black Needles, and The Kiss of the Rainbow Scorpion."

3

From his vantage point on Thunder Butte, José could see most of North and South Dakota. Beyond that he could see Jupiter and Mars. He thought of his great-grandfather, who fled to Saskatchewan in the days before the vortexes, after the Europeans brought their diseases to the Great Plains, and no one, not even fur traders and their wives, were immune. Many of the homesteaders were tormented by memories of unfaithful lovers and blankets of dark, radioactive clouds. The forces of civilization were perceived as a cruel hoax.

4

José's great-grandfather, who homesteaded in Canada, was originally from West Texas, not far from the undocumented territory to the south. He fell into a vortex near El Paso, The Boulder of Unceasing Prayer, then reappeared in the Dakota Badlands, where he wandered for many days in a trance-like state until he reached the banks of the Cheyenne River. Cities were popping up in the foothills of the Mystic Mountains. Herds of antelope and buffalo were spreading like waves across the grasslands. He saw the blue lights of a million souls glowing in the river.

5

All this was foreseen by Marie-Hélène, a French Canadian, who married the great-grandfather of the man who fell in the river when she knew for certain that he was free of the plague. "Even the lives we love most must be sold for land," she said as they planted seeds in the silhouettes of their own hands. "We have all been through a vortex and come out in a new and strange country," she told her husband. "There are many angels in the hills around Thunder Butte. On the darkest nights you can see them all at once, shining in the sky."

Titan's Blue Aura

I can't remember anything—the morning after
or "Radar Love." There is no now here, only music
and lyrics: the laugh track was canceled. The sky
goes pink, then green like a ham sandwich. Is this
a preview of the afterlife? I wonder, gazing out
the window at Titan's blue aura. Song after song
about tinhorn lovers, the sort of people I know
nothing about. On one side of the highway there
is forest, a slow-moving ballet of pine and fir trees,
on the other side an empty building painted black.
And I think how, years ago, I saw an exhibit
of Sioux ghost shirts in a museum in Rapid City
and my dad was standing in the corner smoking
a cigarette and wearing his Napa Auto Parts jacket
and I felt the ghosts right there in the room with me.

Handrail of the Stars

When I'm awake, I'm trying to preserve
the moment, holding the dark clouds

on my fingertips, taking the hills in my arms.
I am not a woman, but I feel the water

in my bones. I see horses falling
like raindrops on the village, soldiers

crawling like ants on the floor of the lodge.
I climb the legs of Red Shirt Table, drop

like a stone through a transparent highway.
Beyond the campfire, elk and buffalo

are grazing in endless prairies. Gone
are the white men, whose hearts burn

like the dead candles of competition.
Nature so pure, the animals are astounded.

II. A Question Mark in a Forest of Snowflakes

War of Independence

"Our only duty to history is to rewrite it."
—Oscar Wilde

1

George Washington was sitting in a bar in Baltimore. He was trying to decide whether or not he should take his army across the Delaware River in small boats. He called Thomas Jefferson, who was sharing a bottle of brandy with his maid, Sally Hemings. Jefferson called Alexander Hamilton, who was cleaning his pistol. "Between the three of us, we should come up with a good plan," Jefferson said. "Let's wager some money," Hamilton said. "I'll bet you Washington can't win without Lafayette's help."

2

And so it was. The French bottled up the English fleet at Yorktown, Cornwallis surrendered, and Jefferson lost the bet. Later, when he heard that Hamilton had lost his duel with Aaron Burr, Jefferson felt a touch of remorse. He was in Paris, drinking cognac with his friend Beaumarchais, who had commissioned 6000 troops to Washington in 1780. Smoke from the bar downstairs rose up through the floorboards and mingled with roses on a small table beside his settee. "Do old soldiers gather on the mountain?" Jefferson wondered.

3

Meanwhile, at Wounded Knee, snow was falling. Crazy Horse was on the phone with Washington who was more than a little concerned about Sitting Bull's inflammatory speech at the Little Big Horn. "I'll send Sherman to Atlanta," the president said, "see what they think down there." At the same time, Lafayette was reading George Custer's book, *My Life on the Plains*, and he didn't believe any of it. He called William Sherman, who had burned his way to Savannah and was standing outside the Park Royale, drinking a bourbon and soda. He was put on hold.

4

On a ridge overlooking the Little Big Horn, Custer was working on his memoirs. "When I get back to Washington and meet with Jefferson," he wrote, "I'll ask about Sherman." Crazy Horse appeared and asked for his scalp, his long yellow hair. Custer refused and the chief headed north to Canada, where he joined Sitting Bull and the Ghost Dancers for their last big hurrah: victory over Washington at Valley Forge.

5

When Sitting Bull looked in the mirror, he saw his grandfather's face. He went outside his tepee, where the Ghost Dancers were preparing for battle. Henry Kissinger was there, with Jill St. John and Zsa Zsa Gabor. "Look, Sitting Bull," Henry said, "I'm sure ve can verk something out. There's no vay you can vin this fight." But Sitting Bull had made his decision. "Last night, I had a vision of white men falling head-first in the snow around Philadelphia," he said. "It is a good day to go skiing."

6

Sally Hemings was spending the weekend at Squaw Valley. She missed Jefferson, who had been appointed ambassador to France. She called Lafayette to see if he knew what Jefferson was up to. "He's up to no good," Lafayette said. "Forget him. *Je t'aime. Je ne pense qu'à toi.*" Sally blushed, but at the same time felt flattered. The day before, while walking along the Potomac, she had seen a halo floating in the river. "What does it mean?" she wondered. "Angels are coming," Lafayette said, "with a terrible swift sword."

7

Meanwhile, at Valley Forge, Washington's men were freezing. They had no shoes and frostbite was a big problem. Washington called Kissinger to see how the negotiations were going. "Not good," Kissinger said. "Sitting Bull cut his meat loaf into thirty pieces last night. He's planning to turn your army into wiener schnitzel." Washington grimaced. He knew he had little chance against a superior force. He told his men to prepare for battle. The rest is history.

Why I Like War

Because it's exciting and dangerous.
Think *Band of Brothers* or *The Longest Day*,
The Thin Red Line, *U-571*, and all the great
films that would not have been made had
there never been a war. Some wars are sexier
than others. Crimean War, Thirty Years War
among the sexiest. Charge of the Light Brigade.
Rocroi, Lützen, Nordlingen. Wow. Vietnam
was one of the least sexy. Dumb strategy.
Short on heroism. Too much dope. Dope
can spoil a war. Stonewall circled the Union
troops at Chancellorsville, rolled up their
flank, got himself killed. Very cool. Stonewall
never got stoned. Dien Bien Phu was more
interesting than the whole ten years the U.S.
squandered in Vietnam. The French know
about sexy wars. Leipzig, Austerlitz, Marengo,
Borodino. They quit fighting when war
stopped being sexy. Aerial bombing. Napalm.
Come on. Get with it. Bring back the infantry
squares and cavalry charges, catapults
and siege towers. Have some fun!

How to Amuse a Tree

Stand very still. Speak in a loud voice.
Flap your arms like you are flying. Confess
your sins. Drink too much coffee. Drive as fast
as you can. Squeal your tires. Run up and down
the street where you live. Do jumping jacks.
Knock yourself out. Tell bad jokes. Contemplate
your navel. Explain the law of gravity. Talk
about the transmigration of souls. Argue about
politics. Hug yourself. Get up early every morning.
Change your clothes every night. Brush your teeth.
Speak softly to birds. Kiss your ass goodbye.
Smoke your last cigarette. Sell your chain saw.
Donate money to the Sierra Club. Stay in one
place for more than a year. Stop wangin' around.
Get a real job. Call your mom. Answer your mail.
Be true to your school. Get aluminum siding.
Climb a mountain. Love a tree. Any tree.

A New Language

An Oregon dictionary: beavers, ducks, big trees,
snow-covered peaks, rocky coastline, umbrellas,
raincoats, fishing rods, paper clips. Bricks like
ships, ships like snowdrifts. The trees do not
forget us. Fog moves in on little Catwoman feet.
There are no centaurs in this forest, the fog says.
Only paintings of Greek philosophers. And big
rubber gloves. We tell the same stories over and
over: the lover who fell asleep when the train
rolled over, the dog that chugged back and forth
between foreign cities. I met her on a Sunday.
Or maybe it was a Monday. She was planning
a trip to New Zealand. Or maybe it was India.
She was the sort of woman who could get your
attention. Already the lake behind my apartment
building was speaking a new language. As she
walked across the street, cars melted like soft cheese.

Reflections on the Revolution in California

Two lakes for the price of one. The wrath of the sea
is overrated. I prefer a double mocha or the shadow
of epistemology. My favorite coffee is called Larry.
Dubuffet did not draw horses or paint Cadillacs.
He preferred life in the Himmelblau. I like spiritual
writing, especially the drug-induced kind. My love
for H. D. is greater than anything written by a minor
poet. If I die tomorrow, do not forget me. Give me
a home where the Communists roam. When we study
the absolute, we ignore our relatives. "Is this real or
unreal?" Byron asked. "Does it have wings?" Dr. Gonzo,
to his credit, brought his machete to the pot bust. San
Francisco was different then. The hair was greener.

The Glass Tulip

We hitchhiked across Ohio, Pennsylvania, New York,
and the tulip fields of Rhodesia. I wanted to be a painter,
but the exhibition was closed. So-and-so's rejection
of history means nothing to me. I prefer the Rose Bowl
in Pasadena. The other folks were in a dilemma. Courbet
had written *The Last Judgment* one stormy day at sea.
When Max Ernst is in town, watch out. Borges took
a bite of his mother's cake and looked out the window.
Barcelona was beginning to bore him. "Some things
exist as they are" seems like good advice. Realism
is overrated. Van Gogh took his toys and went home.
I loved *The Valley of the Dolls*. On the radio, another song,
another three minutes of compressed life. After a period
of reflection, Cubism was an irritation. *The grammar deviates.*
Handle it! Crossing the divide south of Multiplication,
Matisse tripped and spilled his vase of purple flowers.

Lemon Twist

Like a blood clot or Zulu warrior, Teresa of Avila,
Groucho Marx. Like buttocks in space, embryos,
impresarios, honey dew melons sprouting
in the backyard. Psychedelic June. The tickets
blew out the window. A cloud of blue, brown,
and green pointillist brushstrokes. A tic-tac-toe
of colors. Have another lemon twist, the bartender
said. Men and their munitions. Sky like quartz.
A tunnel of blackberries. At the Jell-O farm they
are copping a plea. Time off for good behavior,
the gelatin show-and-go. Picasso and Mondrian
pumping iron. Less like a turnip than a rutabaga.
Blue cabbage revisited, painted red, or stripped
of its fascination. What makes the space dangerous
is academic. I was coming home after a long trip.
It was dark outside. We smoked up the lawn.

Large

She kept calling me David, but that's not my name.
We were walking in the park. There were two or three
Davids there, and a tall guy with cheekbones like fenders,
his feet on fire, ice cream on his breastplate.
One miniature Goliath. He was playing country
music and winking broadly at a signpost. A girl I knew
grew up suddenly.

One of the Davids suggested I buy some tobacco
and sprinkle it on my lawn. Whatever was
in the pouch was more powerful than England
and America—and most of Japan. The grass in my
front yard was transformed into a jungle, inhabited
by enormous blind animals.

The next day, at the courthouse, I saw an old man
and his young companion—the mysterious couple
or "gruesome twosome," as the kids described them.
I decided to communicate in another language,
talk about Lord Byron and the break-out of centrifugal
forces at the laundromat. "But what about
the ocean currents?" one of the lawyers asked.

It seemed like a simple question at the time,
if you consider that legal arguments are wired differently
than the speaking hills. But now, as I write this,
I think he was referring to the "true crossing,"
or the body that has become so
large it feels the wind breathing through it.

We Were Not Born to Forget

Lords and ladies, ladies leaping, lords sitting or tripping
or both. The wind holding its breath. The cat
in the hat is not the cat with the bat. Black coins
pour from a spout in the thing you consider
useless. In Alaska,
it is too late for the dancing longhorns. A young girl,
who is considered missing, is holding a glass of milk.
This time of year, we feel good about everything,
even the craters in the sidewalk.

I could have tripped out D.C., but I've got better things
to do. Read a poem, sing a song, write
a letter to someone new. Peek into the dark drawers
of Mother Money.
The truly hungry eat more than they should. We live
in a world of thoughts, impressions, misperceptions,
and dazzling insights. King Agrippa saw what St. Paul
failed to see: the joke is on us.
Everyone is pretty much living at the same time.

Wrong Number

All the cells in your body are replaced by
new cells every six months. But 95% of your
thoughts are the same. You get one small
cell if you commit a crime. A new cell phone
every year along with a new monthly contract.
A new cellmate every two years, one phone
call for each arrest. One night in jail is like
two hours on hold. Your wife is leaving.
"I've always wanted to go someplace else,"
she says. "I'll call you on my cell phone."
After six months you are a new person.
All your cells have been replaced. But 95%
of your thoughts are the same. Your wife
is still gone. She will come to herself, you think,
and then you realize she is no longer the same
person. All her cells have been replaced.
Your cell phone contract has expired. Your
new cell phone takes pictures. It takes pictures
of you in your cell. Your cellmate is not
your soul mate. In six months he will be
someone else. But not your wife. Wherever
she is. She didn't say where she was going.
You punch in her number. No answer.

Coffee Mountain High

I drank thirty cups of coffee this morning. Just to see if I
could do it. I ran around to different coffee shops: Starbucks,
Coffee Culture, Seattle's Finest, Grindhouse, Java Joe's,
and bought a tray of four *grandés* at each. I count a *grandé*
as one-and-a-half cups. So after five stops I had bought—
and consumed—*thirty cups of coffee.* The first thing I noticed,
sitting in my car at a stoplight, the red light was bigger and
brighter than ever before, and it was pulsing. Next thing I
noticed my thoughts seemed to leapfrog each other. *Where
am I going? Head of steam. All the way to Christmas. I'll be there
in a second.* And so on. I remember reading that the mind of
a Zen master is like a placid pond. Mine was like a percolator.
Thoughts bubbling hard, then hitting a rapid boil. *Can I reduce
the heat? I am not Superman. Is the car still running? Bridge over
troubled water.* And then an amazing thing happened. I felt
calm and wired at the same time. The caffeine had peaked.
Choirs of angels. Maybe I am Superman. Leaping thoughts, so what?
I think I realized then I was going to be OK. My heart would
not stop. My brain would not blow a gasket. I drove to church.
The sermon was on temperance. I was able to sit still for most
of it. Two trips to the men's room. Afterwards I drove home
feeling a little depressed. *Should I stop for a cup? This highway
seems to go on forever. How many stop signs are there?*

This Really Happened

I woke up this morning and my head was missing. I looked every-where: under the bed, in the closet, bathroom, under a pile of clothes on the floor. Where could it be? I tried to recall events of the day before. Lunch at Rodeo Steak House, happy hour at The Happy Hour—or California Club, I forget which, they are side by side—my buddy Boyd and I were drinking boilermakers—and then I drove home blind, up and down twisted canyon roads, one set of wheels on the highway, the other in the weeds. I parked my truck in front of my house and went straight to bed. Or did I? Now I remember. I didn't go home last night. I stopped at the White Horse Inn for a nightcap and Lulu Tubbs was sitting in a booth at the back giving me the big eye. After a few beers, we went to her place, drank a bottle of Old Crow, and everything went black. Wait a minute. That's not what happened. I slept with Lulu a week ago, not last night. I'm sure that's true. Last night, I drove up to Truckee to see Patty Wong and we rode bareback into the high chaparral, swam in her manmade lake, lay on a blanket buck naked in the moonlight. Now I remember. It's all coming back to me. Regrets, I've got a few. My sordid past, my wasted life, my lost head. Lulu. Patty. I miss her horse. Her lake of sin.

A Week of Sundays

On Monday you are walking down a street
that leads nowhere. Flowers are blooming
at the edge of your vision.

On Tuesday you see a woman you know
at a café where you eat lunch at least once
a week. She is not smiling.

On Wednesday you are alone, thank God,
and branches are clawing at the walls
of your house.

On Thursday you fall through a hole in the
floor and land in the basement you never
knew existed.

On Friday you feel more alive than you
felt earlier in the week. You sense that
trees are lining up outside your house.

On Saturday your dog is sick and your horse
fell asleep. You wander here and there,
searching for a lost appointment.

On Sunday you see her again at your
favorite café. You assumed she would love
you forever. You were wrong.

Last Date

No beauty in rattlesnake heaven, the fourth day
of lunch, consecutive anthologies arranged
in complicated . . . sleeping and eating like a bear.
Those who got there last were paid the same,
and this pissed the others off. It's an old story.
There is no witness protection program.
They aren't taking the fall for somebody else,
not even Dick and DeeDee. Remember,
this is the official version, not part of the cover-up.
To be bound by our mistakes is disconcerting,
like sitting around until time vanishes
or taking your car downtown for a bath.
I'm still not sure if they are building a staircase
to Wichita, but I know the trunk is empty.
A blue haze filled the air. I was walking home,
thinking about how much I would miss her.
All summer by myself. Me and Elvis,
the golden jukebox. The awnings of the sea
are too deep. You're invisible wherever you go.

The Twelve Days of Christmas

On the first day of Christmas,
       my true love came to visit.
On the second day of Christmas,
       she complained of a headache.
On the third day of Christmas,
       I sat in my car and listened to music.
On the fourth day of Christmas,
       the car disappeared and the music wrapped
       itself around my body like a cloak.
On the fifth day of Christmas,
       she suggested I dip my tongue
       in a glass of bourbon.
       My tongue is still numb.
On the seventh day of Christmas,
       I dressed in black and walked the streets alone.
On the eighth day of Christmas,
       I drank champagne from my shoe.
       I let my foot stay the night.
On the ninth day of Christmas,
       I was a saint in Indiana or Vermont.
       I did not eat meat or drive a car.
On the tenth day of Christmas,
       I could not stay awake.
       My whole Guggenheim was deranged.
On the eleventh day of Christmas,
       I was a sentence floating on a river,
       a question mark in a forest of snowflakes.
On the twelfth day of Christmas,
       she gestured and the air parted like flowers.
       I was a small fire on the river.
       I ran my fingers through the air.

Forgetting

Ice and snow kicked by the wind,
shouldered against fences, knee-deep

in the center of the highway. Headlights
dim, like stars. Rocks say yes, join us.

I feel the earth underneath, my legs
gone to dust. I am beginning to forget,

flowers blooming around the edges
of my memory. Green lights flickering

in the emergency room. Shadows
on the cemetery wall. Sky like a river,

a red bird perched on the steering wheel.
I take the sun in my hands, the moon

in my arms. Light turns to dark, rapture.
The car sighing, groaning, giving up

the ghost. Saying good-bye to my wife,
picking up my car keys, getting out of bed,

waking up on the last day of my life,
dreaming I would live forever.

III. Red Poppies on the Moon

The Moving House

Our house moves around at night. We're sure
of it. It takes a stroll around the neighborhood,
then returns and settles down on its foundation.
We can feel the house moving. It's sort of cool,
like riding on a train, except there are no clickety-
clacks. The house moves smoothly, as though
it's floating on air, leisurely sailing down one
street, then up another. None of our neighbors
have mentioned our moving house. Mrs. Smedley
hinted she may have seen it trucking past her
house late one night when she couldn't sleep.
"Something very large whisked past my window,"
she said. "And I don't believe it was a car or a truck."
My wife wonders if we should tell someone about
our moving house. "I don't think it's a public
hazard, honey," I say to reassure her. But, to be
honest, I harbor secret doubts. What if the house
decides to move to Kansas or Oklahoma or some
place far away? "I guess we'll cross that bridge
when we come to it," I tell my wife as we settle
in bed for the night. "In the meantime, bon voyage."

Once I Was a Spider-Man

Newspaper headline, a short story, two paragraphs:
"Spider-Man Freed from Legal Web." Flash
back to full-color episodes of the comic book,
mid-Seventies, I was a student in college, Peter Parker
bitten by a radioactive spider. Easy to identify
with his plight, away from home for the first time,
a freshman dreaming every night of living a secret life,
being super-human, climbing the sides of skyscrapers.
And now, expanding the frame, closing my eyes
and seeing the same bright colors I saw years ago,
when I was taking hallucinogenic drugs. Time
stands on end, does a somersault, folds up like
a tent. And suddenly Spider-Man is fifty-seven
and ready to retire. His legal problems forgotten,
he puts some money down on a condo in Puerto Vallarta.
And yet it all seems too confining, he says to himself,
as he drops a web across Wall Street and hops
roof-to-roof to the New York Stock Exchange.

The Secret Lives of Books

1. Call for Help

A call just came in from Shadow Valley Ranch—you know, where they found the twisted candles and some other stuff I can't mention—you remember, that episode where Nancy Drew was trapped in a caved-in mine, and the old man everyone thought was dead came to save her. "No new threats," she said to the guy most scary, but not so much so that anyone would actually feel *afraid*. "OK, I understand," he said and gracefully departed from the warehouse where her pet dog was in a lot of trouble.

2. Something on the Floor

Under the covers at night, I could feel their attraction for each other. D'Artagnan and Milady de Winter. Looking through a keyhole into Richelieu's chambers, I could see that some sordid scene would be played out several times, like in one of those novels by Robbe-Grillet. *There are two windows and one is closed. I see a table, something on the floor, a robe or nightgown.* A few years later, I sat in the same room where Winston Smith tried to conceal his diary from Big Brother. This is what I wrote:

3. Before The Fall

The wind stood still and stared at Chingachgook. *Hey man, I can relate,* was how he put it, the sky unraveling along the spine of a mountain, clouds freezing and falling heavily on a lake. Uncas spoke to his father from inside a tree: *So much blood in the rain from the west. Every story is about The Fall. You are spending way too much time in the woods.*

Hawkeye knows that eventually only the animals will speak his language. Running through the forest, he feels the sun on his face, the earth starting to move.

4. What Happened in Bayport

I was driving home through the valley of the crisscross shadow. Plants that once lined the sides of the highway were now dead. The Hardy Boys hadn't changed much: Frank was a lawyer and Joe a reporter for the *Bayport Times*. They'd heard stories about the melted coins, but hadn't seen any, not a nickel or a dime. We took the Sleuth II for a run up the bay, past a nuclear power plant. A heavy mist enveloped the boat and we were back in the Fifties. Danger was just around the corner, the mark on the door like a silent kiss.

5. A Sacred Gift

When I was a child, I was fascinated by Peter, the goat-boy, who traveled the countryside with his cat, Jules, and his horse, Isaac. In a village in Bavaria, they met Heidi, who was probably thirty, but looked like she was thirteen. Her family was poor, but it didn't matter, because love is money and they had more than they could spend. "What happened to the priest who taught me the ancient wisdom?" Heidi asked Peter. "A sacred gift is never forgotten," he told her. Red birds perched in the tree beside her house. Soon they would turn into apples.

What Large Eyes

"Not my Grandma," she said, and dropped her custard.
The wolf could run pretty fast. How dark
it was inside him, and so strange, like a cave.
Listen to how it sounds: the traffic and high-pitched
call of the wolf. On Central Park West,
a large church but no steeple. Here
the villains are drawn like stick figures
in your favorite book. Under the bed,
your best friends have come to stay.
They march up and down single-file or sleep in a heap.
Remnants of winter, the kindness of Father Christmas,
your brother Jeff joking about Grandma's
homemade pie. In the far distance,
the Alaskan wolf wears white clothes.

Just Like Paul Bunyan

One summer, a few years ago, I went back to the farm where I grew up. I couldn't believe how much things had changed. My parents' house had shrunk to the size of a toaster oven. I was dumfounded.

"I can't believe I grew up here," I said to my wife.

"It must be those vitamins you've been taking," she said. "You've grown so much bigger than when you were a child. Everything looks smaller."

I looked down at the house. I could crush it, I thought, with one foot. Or I could kick it like a football into the nearby river. I thought back to a night when I was a child and my mother read Paul Bunyan stories before I fell asleep. I imagined Paul and Babe the Blue Ox standing outside the house, as big as skyscrapers. And here I was, twenty years later, looking down at the house where I grew up.

I wondered if Mom and Dad were still there. I knelt and looked in the window. Yes, there was Mom in the kitchen, wearing an apron and baking a pie. Dad was listening to the radio and washing dishes. I stood up quickly. "What are we going to do?" I asked my wife. "A large animal could come along and knock the house over."

She shrugged. "I don't know, honey. Maybe we should take the house with us."

"OK," I said and picked up the house and put it in the car.

As we drove back to the city, I wondered what would become of Mom and Dad. Would they live out the rest of their days in their tiny house? "Don't worry," my wife said. "We'll keep it in the family room. It'll be safe there."

And she was right. Mom and Dad passed on a few years later, after our daughter was born, and now she uses their house as a dollhouse. Every now and then I look in the window and think about those great pies Mom made. And I remember Dad sitting in his miniature living room smoking his pipe and reading *True Crime* magazine.

"Do you think they were afraid of us," my daughter asked.

"Oh no," I said. "To them we were good friends, just like Paul Bunyan and Babe the Blue Ox."

Moses—the Early Years

Moses is walking along the beach with Rabbi Eleazar, a tall man with a long black beard. There are white birds in his beard, and when he looks at Moses, stars are floating in his eyeballs. The rabbi is very thin—he has been living on watercress and snakeroot for forty-five years. His teeth are yellow from smoking unfiltered cigarettes.

"Moses," the rabbi says. "It is time for you to go off on your own and learn the ways of the world." But Moses feels afraid and doesn't want to do any public speaking. "I'd rather die," he says.

They squat on the sand and share a yellow cigarette. The rabbi is becoming irritated. He is thinking about roast beef and mashed potatoes. "Master," Moses says, "please tell me what lies ahead. Will I be famous? Will I make money? Will I find true love?"

"None of the above," the rabbi says. "You will carry a big staff through the desert. You will meet many people smarter than yourself. And when you die, no one will understand your thoughts."

"So what's the point?" Moses wonders.

"It's not about points, but circles and squares. The door of the temple will be torn like paper. And when you see the truth, angels will bring wings to carry you beyond your body. And when you finally stop to rest, the blessings you bestow on others will light up like neon signs."

"Is that good?" Moses asks.

"It is neither good nor bad," the rabbi says, birds fluttering in his beard. "Here, have another cigarette." This one is blue, with a small anchor printed on the paper. "Use that anchor to cast yourself beyond the Shekinah, and when you get to the other side, tell them, 'Johnny Boy is here.'"

The rabbi vanishes, and Moses stares at his cigarette. He has a lot to think about.

The Advance Gardening Memoranda

In the beginning, the powers of rejuvenation
were like an electric storm, conveying
a new sense of significance to Ecclesiastes,
hung in the bay like a carousel of deserted highways.
A wall of black arches circled the square.
Pastel cataracts lined the river above the falls,
colossal stone monuments rose up
from the streambed. After years of pessimism,

the inhabitants had become fascinated
with drab colors and wasted time.
The trick was in the ignition and bound up visually
in the economics of space: a log cabin popped
from the toaster like a salt shaker run amok.
The horizon took on another dimension,
like a cave of light—
or coves hemmed in by nylon fences.

Beads of water hit the fan. The hair on the giant's
chest was no longer matted, gone awash,
or drip-dried. The prime minister of monotony,
at first spellbound by the terrorist mystique,
then inundated by a wave of ennui,
was suddenly nipped in midair and flung
like a crystal harpoon through the eye of a dream.
The back door opened, and nothing solid walked in.

Alms for the Poor

The doorbell rings. It's my friend, Pierre. He is bourgeois.
"Welcome," I say. I am bourgeois, too. We are both bourgeois.
In fact, everyone in this neighborhood is bourgeois.
Pierre thinks that being bourgeois is a bad thing,
even though I give alms to the poor every Sunday
at my bourgeois church. Pierre, who is both bourgeois
and anti-bourgeois, gives nothing to the poor. He does
not attend church. We sit and drink tea silently as if we
do not disagree about anything. I shut my eyes and when
I open them again, instead of Pierre sitting across from me,
I see a leather purse. I open the purse. It is full of gold coins.

American Spirit

On the ground is an empty pack of American Spirit cigarettes. The master has quit smoking, but the mistress hasn't. For her, it's an act of rebellion. I walk past their bedroom on my way to the kitchen. The master's shoes are next to the bed—for a quick getaway, I surmise, although the heat right now has addled my brain. I reach the end of a long corridor. In a room to my right, a small boy, who looks like Huckleberry Finn, is sitting in front of a television sucking his thumb. I find the kitchen, blend two daiquiris, place them on a tray with a box of water biscuits and head back through the labyrinth. I place the tray on a metal table under a pink umbrella. The flower box on the windowsill is divided into triangles in the same manner as the blue robe the mistress wears to the pool. She pauses beside the diving board, tosses her robe on a chair. Like a wet towel, the afternoon over, under, upside-down. She cuts the water without a splash.

Turnpike

This quiet in me is just the beginning. Silence will follow
me all the days of my life. Salt on the freeway. A tonic
for the underbelly of life. Bring a candle when you come.
And I said, I have no upstairs or downstairs, only a long
hallway into the next season, a village of back alleys,
dreams of Calcutta or Cairo, crowded streets, beggars,
the ghosts of Brahmins and pharaohs. I see no shadows,
only a dry ocean in every direction. I have fallen asleep
when I needed most to stay awake. The highway was
yanked out from under the car and we were flung
like rag dolls across a field of ice. In all the turnpikes
of America are frozen cars, the dead limping into the
next life. Young gods racing their chariots to Valhalla,
Chillicothe, the rainbow cities along the Nile. Each sweet
dream is a love story. I'll pay my toll only once.

Agents of the Prince

On the playground, men in dark coats hurried past
the swings and monkey bars. This gift, they said,
is a box you may never open, but keep it with you
always. In the morning, snow gripped the shadows
of trees. Things that once seemed familiar were now
abstract or altered beyond recognition: the house
where I grew up, maps of torn buildings, tattered
streets. I stood at the window and breathed deeply.
A flock of sparrows flew past into the light, ethereal
mist that sat on the house like a cupcake. Windows
were erased and doors reprogrammed. We entered
through a mirror, caught our breath, let it go again.
At noon, agents of the prince appeared, asked where
they could find the *brujo*. His name was an alphabet
of blighted orchards, a fever of diseased air.

Beginning of Summer

Rain is like a night-blooming cactus,
a white blossom visible through a frozen
windshield. The dead pitch their tents
in the land of the living, in the flowers
that fall like rainbows on a river
of Chinese willows. In this country,
wisdom can be found everywhere,
in books and paintings, in the thunder's
silent echo. Life is like a flame burning
in red pigment, a sentence erased
from a final chapter. Nothing exists
except the morning sky and another
cold, cloudy day. Too much sun,
too much rain. Too many shadows
and empty coats, abandoned farms.
My dog ran down to the river, coyotes
howled, the sun set in a slow and lazy
moment. Sheets of water like broken
orchids. Red poppies on the moon.
Silver raindrops on a stone wall.
At the beginning of summer, a vote
is taken: sunlight is always the winner.

Strange Artifacts

Houses to the north part of a body of information,
a point where one reaches for something, the other
invokes the name of her special god. It is only a matter
of recollection, another city, a heated room, blue shadows
on the road to some snowbound place. Try to think of this
as a kind of music, a glass jar, or a friend masquerading
as someone else, not someone you know, but someone
you should know, a neighbor or friend of a close friend.
You hear a song on the radio that has some special meaning,
brings back a moment when you are sitting in a restaurant
listening to "Lara's Theme" or "Moon River" and snow is
piling up in great swollen drifts, and she is saying, "When
I think of you I see a farm in the Midwest or a cattle ranch
in Wyoming." But it is not you she is thinking of, and
the hills are moving closer and in the ground are strange
artifacts, and what she really sees is a cave of red light.
"I know you were angry, snowing all the way home."

Between the Body and the Window
Is Another Revelation

They do not understand the purity of dreams or how night
envelops the sleeper. The waiters and maids remember me
and the students are riding elevators that stop at different
levels of consciousness. In the first dream we are all one
and everything is perfect. The elevator is not enclosed so
we can see the stars flowing like a river around the sleeping
buildings. Released from thoughts of rivers and buildings,
dreams fly out the windows. Stars fall on the floor,
drift against the walls. The bed is a half moon dreaming.
I could not distinguish one dream from another. I've hung
around outside these places for years, hoping they would
eventually let me in, hoping they would take me into
their dream world, but they never do. From a different
perspective, the buildings change, but the desire to be
taken care of remains the same. Health, holiness, healing
completely natural and dependable. A view of the stars.
Venice. A village on the Nile. White Christmas.

No Longer Dust

There isn't much to worry about: the first fruits
have been held over for a new planting. Thickets
of cottonwood and mimosa leaf from an era
when almost everything organic was disavowed.
A skeleton buried inside a closet of cinnamon trees.
At night I watch doves fly across the moon,
feel my breath escaping as butterflies wave
their feathery fans inside a dreamer's daily prayer.
Blue herons follow me home from school,
nest in the garden below my bedroom window.
It is soft, so soft, the blanket around my shoulders,
a largo of islands and ocean currents flowing
north to the Bering Sea, across the strait into a song
of time and memory, veering north, turning white,
like a star inside a temple, a violin speaking
its first word. Then back to the outside world,
where the breath of sacrifice is creating a new being.
Her name is forest, pond, or mud, the percussion
of silver on a glass roof, ice smoldering in sleep.
Clarity where none can be found. Earth sinking,
then rising like a blade of light, a weed planted in
a painting of blessed soil. No longer dust, but stardust.

The End of Time

Red peonies on the table. White lilies floating in the air.
It furthers one to consult the Great Spirit, analyze
paperback novels, catch a sunspot, climb a falling star.
At the base of the tree a golden node. Grief disappears,
a spider stretches its legs, yawns. You take the blue
needle in your hand, stitch a smile in the clouds.
A man who loved too much ate an orange on a dark
night. Under a cinnamon tree. A woman who had too
much to drink washed out to sea. A man who drove
too fast sped into the future, bought an airplane.
Where time ends space begins. Light bends. My paper
crane flew away. I found the missing ring in a foot
of snow. One blunder is as good as the next: after
twenty years everything seems strange. He brandished
his sword. I brandished my bottle. What is to become
of the outlaw substance? Does memory transform
hearing into something else? Like a blue ship sailing
into red water, the dream of dying is gone.

About the Author

Michael Malan is editor of *Cloudbank*, a literary journal published in Corvallis, Oregon. His poems and flash fiction have been published in *Epoch, Denver Quarterly, Potomac Review, Poetry East, Hayden's Ferry Review, South Carolina Review, CutBank, Wisconsin Review, Rhino, The Christian Science Monitor,* and elsewhere.

CPSIA information can be obtained
at www.ICGtesting.com
Printed in the USA
FSOW01n0046020317
31274FS